BESIDE THE STILL WATERS

Lord, lead me beside the still waters!
  Oh, give me peace within
For troubles like billows surround me
  And hide what might have been.

Lord, lead me! Lead me! Lead me
  Beside the still waters that flow
Through shady green pastures of peace, sweet peace
  Where true faith and courage grow.

Lord, lead me where hope springs eternal,
  Where truth shines bright and clear;
Oh, give but one taste of their sweetness
  And I shall never fear.

Lord, lead me beside the still waters
  And there restore my soul;
Oh, help me make Thy will and Thy way
  My one — my only goal.

Lord, lead me! Lead me! Lead me
  Beside the still waters that flow
Through shady green pastures of peace, sweet peace
  Where true faith and courage grow.

Beside Still Waters

(Poems to Comfort and Encourage)

by

PHYLLIS C. MICHAEL

Illustrated by Judith A. Michael

ZONDERVAN PUBLISHING HOUSE
GRAND RAPIDS   MICHIGAN

Copyright © 1969 by Phyllis C. Michael.
All rights reserved. No portion of this book or the illustrations may be reproduced in any way without written permission of the publisher.
Grateful appreciation is expressed to the following for permission to use poems owned by them:

Singspiration Inc. — for "God Is There," Copyright © 1961 Singspiration Inc.; "Across the Great Divide," "God Is," "In the Valley of Tears," "Just Beyond the Shadows," "Safe in His Care," "Some Bright Tomorrow," and "With a Song in My Heart," Copyright © 1969 Singspiration Inc.

The Rodeheaver Co. for "At the End of the Road," "God Answers Prayer," "The Touch of His Hand," and "Beside the Still Waters" Copyright © 1969 The Rodeheaver Co.

The publisher is also grateful for permission to quote the following poems which are slated to appear in Ideals — "By Faith," "One Day at a Time," "Why Worry?"

First printing	February 1969
Second printing	November 1969
Third printing	1970
Fourth printing	1971

Library of Congress Catalog Card Number 69-11636
Printed in the United States of America

to
My Husband

TABLE OF CONTENTS

Across the Great Divide	9
As If	10
As Time Rolls On	11
At the End of the Road	12
Because I Could Not See Him	13
Beyond	14
Beyond All This	15
Both the Sun and the Rain	16
By Faith	17
Doesn't God Care?	18
Feet of Clay	19
Forward	20
God Answers Prayer	21
God's Garden	22
God Knows What's Best	23
God Loves You	24
God Is	25
God Is There	26
God's Larger Plan	27
God's Plan	28
God's Symphony	29
Heartache Hill	30
He Cares	31
He Fills My Cup	32
He Is Near	33
How Can I Doubt?	34

How Often	35
In Green Pastures	36
In the Valley of Doubt	37
In the Valley of Tears	38
I Prayed a Prayer	39
It's Never Easy	40
Just Beyond the Shadows	41
Just One Day at a Time	42
Let Go and Let God	43
Lord, I Believe	44
My Guide, My Light	45
My Ship Must Wait	46
Not All We Ask	47
Not Mine to Ask	48
One Day at a Time	49
Perhaps Not All	50
Safe in His Care	51
Sail On	52
Ship Ahoy!	53
Some Bright Tomorrow	54
The Answered Prayer	55
These Must Be Bought	56
The Touch of His Hand	57
Thy Will Be Done, O Lord	58
Why Not Take It All to Jesus?	59
Why Worry?	60
With a Song in My Heart	61
Who Am I?	62

ACROSS THE GREAT DIVIDE

When I put out to sail the sea
   Across the Great Divide,
My heart shall have no fear, no dread
   For I have faith — inside.

I know I shall not sail alone
   Nor shall I lose the way;
My Pilot shall be with me then
   Just as He is today.

When I put out to sail the sea,
   Let faith fill your heart, too,
For somewhere on that other shore —
   I'll watch and wait — for you.

AS IF

Act as if the world were kind,
  The skies no longer gray,
As if the sun were shining through,
  The clouds all rolled away.
Act as if your heart were full
  Of peace and love and song,
As if not anything at all
  Could ever have gone wrong.

Yes, act "as if" and soon you'll see
  Some wisdom in this plan;
You'll see that *nothing* seems as bad
  As when you first began.
Just smile and *make* this world grow kind,
  Make someone's sky less gray;
Make someone's sun shine through just now
  And yours will, too, some day.

AS TIME ROLLS ON

As Time rolls on
God gives us grace
To accept the things
that come our way,
To live with them
and calmly face
The joys and griefs
of each new day.

Faith never comes
with a surge of power
At a moment's notice
like the wind that blows,
Nor yet in the stillness
of a midnight hour —
But as Time rolls on —
slowly it grows.

God gives us grace
to forget some things,
To see only the rainbow
when the storm is gone.
Oh, greatest, indeed,
of the blessings life brings —
God gives us *faith*
as Time rolls on.

AT THE END OF THE ROAD

There are blessings unknown I can call all my own
When I come to the end of the way;
There's a wonderful Friend who lives just 'round the bend
And He'll be there to meet me that day.

At the end of the road! At the end of the road!
Jesus waits at the end of the road;
He has gone to prepare me a home over there
And He waits at the end of the road.

In this royal abode at the end of the road
There are treasures, I'm told, oh so rare;
And I'll see face to face by God's wonderful grace
All my friends waiting, too, over there.

More than this none can tell, but I'm sure all is well —
I shall be with my Saviour one day;
When I reach Borderland, He will give me His hand
And my home is just one step away.

There is nothing to fear, let there be not one tear
When I come to this earth's last long mile;
For my Saviour will wait there beside heaven's gate
And He'll welcome me home with a smile.

At the end of the road! At the end of the road!
Jesus waits at the end of the road;
He has gone to prepare me a home over there
And He waits at the end of the road.

BECAUSE I COULD NOT SEE HIM

Because I could not see Him,
I said there was no God;
And then, one day, came illness
And paths I once had trod
Waited in vain for my footsteps,
Waited and looked up to God.

I waited, too, and waited!
I, too, looked up to God,
And while lying there I saw Him
Push through the dark brown sod,
In the form of a pure white lily —
I touched it — the handwork of God.

At last I came to know that
God is everywhere,
He's in the buds and blossoms,
He's even in the air;
Although I could not see Him,
I knew that He was there.

Now as I look about me,
I can't quite understand,
But I never can deny Him
For I've felt the touch of His hand;
I know that He is with me
And things are just as He planned.

BEYOND

Beyond your ev'ry heartache,
Beyond your ev'ry care,
Our blessed Lord is waiting —
I know you'll find Him there.

Beyond your ev'ry sorrow,
Beyond your deepest need,
There's One who's always willing
Your hungry soul to feed.

How sweet to lean on Jesus,
To go to Him in prayer;
Beyond your ev'ry heartache,
I know you'll find Him there.

BEYOND ALL THIS

Though thorns infest the very ground
   My aching feet must tread;
Though clouds hang low, yes, all around
   And fill my heart with dread,

Still, still, O Lord, my song shall be.
   I'll trust! I'll trust in Thee!
Still, still, O Lord, my song shall be,
   I'll trust! I'll trust in Thee.

Though mountains rise so steep, so high
   They seem to bar my way;
Ah, yes, indeed, though earth, though sky
   Shall crumble yet this day,

Still, still, O Lord, I'll trust in Thee;
   I know Thou lovest me!
Still, still, O Lord, I'll trust in Thee;
   I know Thou lovest me.

BOTH THE SUN AND THE RAIN

I once asked the Lord to withhold from my world
    The clouds, the winds, and the rain;
I asked Him to take from my life for all time
    All suff'ring, all sorrow, all pain.

God answered my prayer — I knew that He would —
    But oh, there was much I forgot!
Without the dark clouds, the cool winds, and the rain,
    The earth became parched and so hot
Earth's blossoms soon faded, its fruit withered, too.
    At last I discovered how wise,
How good was the way God meant things to be —
    Both the sun *and* the rain we must prize.

BY FAITH

There are many things I do not know
  But I can feel God's love;
Though all about me seems unfair,
  I'll trust in Him above.

There are many things I cannot see
  They're not revealed to man;
But I have faith in One who cares.
  And in His perfect plan.

There are many things I cannot tell —
  Just how I know God's real;
But, oh, what joy to walk with Him,
  By *faith* content to feel.

DOESN'T GOD CARE?

To me! To me! Tell me why to me!
   Why did it happen to me?
Doesn't God care? Has He ceased to exist?
   Why does this grief have to be?

I've asked this same question a thousand times,
   I've prayed, "Not to me," o'er and o'er;
And then, just today, the true answer came —
   "God loves whom He chastens — more."

To me! To me! Tell me why to me!
   Why did it happen to me?
The Master has work for me to do,
   That's why this grief must be.

Like gold refined and freed from its dross,
   My life must be purged and made pure
For only by walking with pain can one learn
   To seek the things which endure.

FEET OF CLAY

Feet of clay! Feet of clay!
   Man has but feet of clay —
A heart of gold and love untold,
   But hands and feet of clay.

I took my eyes from God one day
   And looked to man alone —
A certain man, a Christian man,
   Like one you may have known.

This man was faithful, kind and good
   As good as he *could* be;
But as I looked I saw he, too,
   Had feet like you and me.

Feet of clay! Feet of clay!
   Man has but feet of clay —
A heart of gold and love untold,
   But hands and feet of clay.

I've learned that I must keep my eyes
   Turned always toward the Lord
If I would find the perfect path
   That leads to sweet accord.

For only God has perfect love,
   The same both night and day —
A heart divine, not cast like mine,
   Nor hands and feet of clay.

FORWARD

I cannot turn backward —
I must go on
O'er rugged mountain steeps;
  Oh, would that I could
    undo certain things,
    But Yesterday's key —
    God keeps.

I cannot turn backward,
    what's done is done,
But somehow there's faith
    in my heart
    For God has given
    this brand new day
    And said,
"Well, now, let's start."

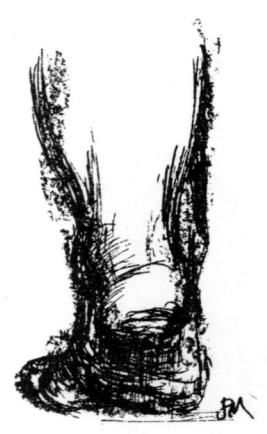

GOD ANSWERS PRAYER

Long, long ago I kneeled to pray;
I thought I knew the words to say.
My heart cried out in new born woe,
"O precious Lord, this can't be so!"
The teardrops fell like autumn rain;
It seemed just then I prayed in vain.
But now I see, yes, now I see —
God, in His wisdom, answered me.

God answers prayer! God answers prayer!
Just put your all in His dear care;
He'll look beyond this day and then
He'll send the answer to your prayer.

There comes a time in ev'ry life
When we are torn by grief and strife;
We cry, "O Lord, why is this so?"
If you have prayed, you know, you know!
It seems to you God will not hear,
It seems just then He's nowhere near;
But this I know, there's good in store,
Just wait and see — just trust Him more.

If you have reached the bridge of doubt
And all seems dark within, without,
Ask God to lead until the dawn —
Pray on in faith, pray on, pray on.
He'll grant your wish or send you grace
To meet what comes to take its place;
Then rest assured, if God says, "No,"
It's all because He loves you so.

God answers prayer! God answers prayer!
Just put your all in His dear care;
He'll look beyond this day and then
He'll send the answer to your prayer.

GOD'S GARDEN

God works in His garden, I'm told, ev'ry day
With the roses He needs for His heav'nly bouquet.

There are times when He picks all the withered, the old,
And gathers them lovingly into His fold.

There are times when He prunes where some other must
  grow
That He on the weak ones more strength may bestow.

But some days He chooses the fairest in sight;
He needs certain buds to make heaven look bright.

How sweet, oh how beautiful is His bouquet!
God works in His garden and best is His way.

GOD KNOWS WHAT'S BEST

I would not ask, dear Father,
   You take the thorns away
From ev'ry little rosebush
   Nor yet from my own day.

For then I should not treasure
   The redness of the rose
Or even all the perfume
   Of ev'ry flower that grows.

Perchance I'd run too swiftly
   If feet were light and free,
And beauty all around us
   My eyes would fail to see.

I simply ask, dear Father,
   "Oh, give me grace to bear
The thorns You feel are needful,
   Yes, even grief and care."

GOD LOVES YOU

No matter how long the way,
No matter how gray the day —
    God loves you.

No matter how steep the height,
No matter how dark the night —
    God loves you.

No matter how great the pain,
No matter how hard the rain —
    God loves you.

Lay aside ev'ry doubt, ev'ry fear;
In this thought sweetly rest, "God is near!"
    God loves you.

There's a purpose behind ev'ry loss,
There's a crown just beyond ev'ry cross —
    God loves you.

Forget things you think *might* have been,
Raise your head, walk by faith once again —
    God *loves you.*

GOD IS

Some things are hard to understand
   And harder still to bear;
But oh, how sweet to know God is
   About us ev'rywhere.

How sweet to know His way is best —
   To make His will our own
And calmly trust His tender care
   The future all unknown.

Some things are hard to understand
   And to accept as right;
But rest assured no joy or grief
   Escapes God's precious sight.

He sees beyond the secret veil.
   He knows tomorrow's needs;
So put your hand in His just now
   And follow where He leads.

GOD IS THERE

When I need a Friend to tell my troubles to,
    God is there, GOD is there;
When I need a Friend to give me strength anew,
    God is there, GOD is there.

When I need a Friend to care when I'm distressed,
    God is there, GOD is there:
When I need a Friend to help me do my best,
    God is there, GOD is there.

When I need a Friend to guide me through the night,
    God is there, GOD is there;
When I need a Friend to make my pathway bright,
    God is there, GOD is there.

    God is there, *always* there,
With a helping hand to lift my load of care;
He'll be faithful to the end, on His promise I depend,
When I really need a Friend — God is there.

GOD'S LARGER PLAN

God answers, "No," sometimes it seems —
   He's answered, "No," to me.
In fact I thought once long ago
   God could not hear or see.

The things I asked seemed quite all right
   And fair — at least just then.
I prayed and prayed, but all in vain
   For God said, "No," again.

The years have passed and now I see
   Why God said, "No," that day;
His way was better far I'm sure —
   I'm glad He bid me, "Stay!"

God sees earth's veil from over there,
   Each man needs gray, then red;
Somehow within God's larger plan
   I, too, must weave my thread.

GOD'S PLAN

I do not understand by half
   God's perfect plan for man;
How can these human eyes of mine
   See things the Master can?

How can a bird that flies tell *us*
   What keeps *him* in the air?
How can a bush which bears a rose
   Define its perfume rare?

How can a tree whose leaves turn gold
   Decipher this at all?
How can the sun describe its rays,
   The rain its drops that fall?

How can the spring so small explain
   The crystal stream that flows?
How can a grain of ripened wheat
   ~~More~~ Make clear the way *it* grows?

Ah, yes, I do not understand,
   But this I know, God holds
Within His hand a plan for all
   As each new day unfolds.

GOD'S SYMPHONY

God ever keeps a watchful eye
    Upon the world below;
There is no grief beyond His sight,
    No care He does not know.

There is no prayer He fails to hear
    Or fails to answer soon;
But sometimes He must say, "Not yet!
    All earth must be in tune!"

This world's a kind of symphony,
    We mortals violins;
The Great Conductor knows the score,
    The note where each begins.

He knows some folks must rest awhile,
    Must listen night and day
Until their hearts find peace within —
    Until they learn His way.

He knows which folks play melody
    In tones flute-like and clear
And which must play the harmony
    To make it sweet to hear.

God ever keeps a watchful eye!
    Have faith! Just wait His cue!
Then play with all your heart and soul
    The part God gives to you.

HEARTACHE HILL

I found the Master on Heartache Hill,
Alone when all was dark and still.

He came to me in my hour of trial;
Together we walked, yes, mile after mile

Till we reached the Valley of Peace below
Where streams of living water flow.

There He restored my soul at last;
Now I am free — all my grief is past.

Nor do I regret all that took me there
To that certain spot in my hour of despair

For I found the Master on Heartache Hill;
Now I am happy — doing His will.

HE CARES

I know that I can trust the Lord
    To keep the stars in place,
To grant the lark, the rose, the oak
    His wisdom and His grace.

I know that I can trust the Lord
    To send the morning light,
To turn each winter into spring,
    To rule each depth, each height.

I know that ev'rywhere I look
    I see His guiding hand,
More beauty, mercy, love, and faith
    Than I can understand.

Then why should I refuse to trust
    Those things I cannot see
To Him who knows tomorrow's needs?
    He cares for you and me.

HE FILLS MY CUP

I never kneel to pray at night
    But that I rise to feel
At peace at last — the world's all right —
    For I know God is real.

I never pause to ask for bread
    To meet some daily need
But that I know I shall be fed —
    Each cry my Lord will heed.

Ah yes, sometimes God sends some things
    Quite different from my thought;
But always in His way He brings
    The good I *should* have sought.

He fills my cup right to the brim,
    His love He always shares;
I never kneel to pray to Him
    But that I find He cares.

HE IS NEAR

When your pathway seems the steepest,
When your sorrow seems the deepest,
Cast your ev'ry care on Jesus —
He is near.

When your broken heart needs mending,
When the night seems never ending,
Tell your Saviour all about it —
He is near.

He will help you climb your mountain,
He has drunk from grief's own fountain,
Rest assured He understands you —
He is near.

He can see beyond your sorrow,
Trust His love until tomorrow,
He has wisely planned your future —
He is near.

HOW CAN I DOUBT?

How can I ever doubt God is
   When all around I see
The wonders of the universe
   God made for you and me?

How can I ever doubt God's love
   When time and time again
His mercy has been shown to me —
   Ah, yes, and to all men!

How can I ever grieve my Lord?
   How can I fail to praise
When day by day He shows His love
   In oh, so many ways?

How can I fear? How can I doubt?
   What else have I beside?
God holds the key, the only key
   That rules both Time and Tide.

HOW OFTEN

How often, oh, how very often
   God has heard my cry;
In the midst of distress He has come to me —
   I have felt Him there nearby.

How often, oh, how very often
   I've needed His guiding hand
When the hill grew far too rough and steep
   And things were not as I planned.

How often, oh, how very often
   He has met my ev'ry need;
When the sky grew dark and I could not see,
   I cried unto Him, "Lord, lead!"

Yet how often, oh, how very often
   I have forgotten this
When once again the dawn has come
   And life is full of bliss.

IN GREEN PASTURES

Green pastures! O Lord, in green pastures please guide me;
I've climbed oh, so long life's steep hill.
Green pastures! O Lord, walk daily beside me;
Teach me Thy precepts, Thy will.

The earth holds no peace, no real pleasure without Thee;
I need Thee, I need Thee just now!
Green pastures, at last, where my heart shall not doubt Thee
Nor question the why or the how.

Green pastures! In mercy, oh, take Thou my hand, Lord!
Lead me, oh, lead me this day
By waters, still waters, where Faith shall command, Lord!
Lead me, oh lead me, I pray!

IN THE VALLEY OF DOUBT

I, too, have been there in the Valley of Doubt
Where life seemed a burden within and without.

I, too, have been there and I know how you feel,
Yet I know in my heart, yes, I know God is real.

Each time that I've been there my lips called His name;
Then swiftly, so swiftly the Good Master came.

He walked right beside me by night and by day,
Right through the dark Valley of Doubt all the way.

New hope filled my heart, true faith lingered on;
At last ev'ry trace of my burden was gone.

I, too, have been there in the Valley of Doubt!
Won't you call on the Saviour? He'll lead you out —

Out into the sunshine, yes, far from your woe —
I, too, have been there and I know — I know.

IN THE VALLEY OF TEARS

In care there is joy, in pain there is peace
    If only we learn to look up;
The mercies and goodness of God never cease —
    True blessings o'erflow from His cup.

In the Valley of Tears! In the Valley of Tears!
God is there in the Valley of Tears!
Just look up, look to Him though His light may seem dim —
God is there in the Valley of Tears.

In want there is hope, in loss there is love —
    Each gift God provides in His way;
There's need for the rain He sends from above,
    There's need for His care ev'ry day.

In doubt there is faith, in grief there is God —
    He loves whom He chastens, I know;
I've felt o'er and o'er both His staff and His rod,
    Through each all His love He'll bestow.

In the Valley of Tears! In the Valley of Tears!
God is there in the Valley of Tears!
Just look up, look to Him though His light may seem dim —
God is there in the Valley of Tears.

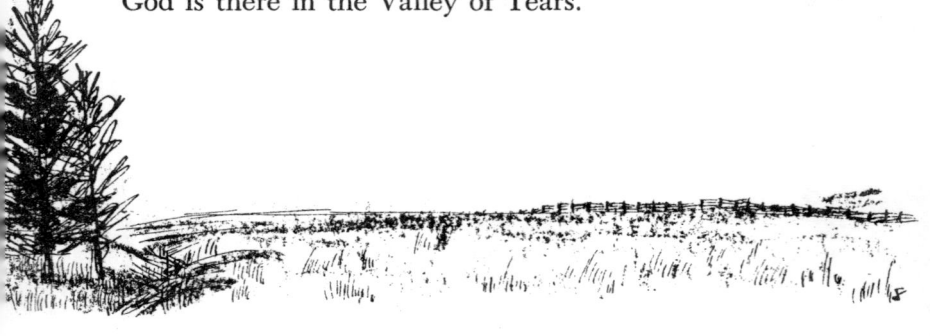

I PRAYED A PRAYER

I prayed a prayer into the night,
I sent it heav'nward out of sight;
The answer soon came back to me,
But oh, so diff'rent from my plea!
At first 'twas hard to understand,
It seemed so far from what I planned;
But now I see God's way was best —
Within His arms, secure, I rest.

God sees much more than we can see,
He knows what is and what's to be;
From here we see a cross to bear,
God sees the crown from over there.
So, walk by faith and not by sight,
Trust God to choose, He knows the right;
His very best you shall receive —
This I believe, *this* I believe.

IT'S NEVER EASY

It's never easy when one must go
    And one must stay — behind;
It's never easy, I know, I know —
    It sears both heart and mind.

It's never easy, but go one must
    When comes the day, the hour;
It's never easy, but if we trust,
    God will give strength and power.

It's never easy! God knows this, too;
    That's why He stays quite near
To help us as we stumble through
    The vale of grief and fear.

It's never easy, but take God's hand
    And pray till night has passed;
Just trust nor ask to understand —
    And peace will come — at last.

JUST BEYOND THE SHADOWS

Just beyond the shadows, there's a ray of light,
'Tis the love of Jesus shining through the night;
Look beyond the shadows, you will find Him there,
Just beyond the shadows waiting for your prayer.

Just beyond the shadows, there's a Helping Hand,
He will guard and guide you, He will understand;
Look beyond the shadows, look to One who's true,
Just beyond the shadows, there's new hope for you.

Just beyond the shadows, there's a Friend who cares,
Ev'ry single burden, ev'ry grief He shares;
Look beyond the shadows, look to God above,
Just beyond the shadows you will find His love.

JUST ONE DAY AT A TIME

One day at a time! Just one day at a time —
That's all I need to live
For God in His infinite wisdom has planned
His mercy thus to give.

One day at a time! Just one day at a time!
I need not pass the gate
And walk within the great unknown
That holds tomorrow's fate.

One day at a time! Just one day at a time!
New strength God shall provide
For ev'ry thing that day shall bring —
He's walking by my side.

LET GO AND LET GOD

Let go and let God
decide
what is best;
Trust in His love,
in Him
sweetly rest.
Though waters may cover
the sea
and the land
They rise or divide
by the touch
of His hand;
Though mountains grow rugged
and valleys
grow deep,
Just walk with the Lord,
your watch
He will keep.

Let the sky that's above you
be cloudy
and gray,
He has a purpose,
so give Him
His way.
Let go and let God
decide
what is best;
Trust in His love,
in Him
sweetly rest.

LORD, I BELIEVE

Though all I feared has come at last
   And my heart is torn by grief,
It's true, it's true, "Lord, I believe,
   Help Thou my unbelief!"

All through this present darkened hour,
   Please, *please* be ever near
To help me banish waves of doubt,
   To help me conquer fear.

This, too, shall pass, I know, I know
   As midnight turns to dawn;
Soon I shall see the light ahead
   But now, just now, lead on.

Yes, all I feared has come at last —
   It seems there's no relief;
But still, oh, still, "Lord, I believe,
   Help Thou my unbelief!"

MY GUIDE, MY LIGHT

I do not know what lies ahead;
But this I know, no fear, no dread
Shall rule my heart though dark the night
For Jesus is my Guide, my Light.

What need have I to see the way
Beyond the bend — beyond this day?
Sufficient this, my Lord shall lead;
His love shall fill my ev'ry need.
I hear His voice within my breast;
He says, "Come unto me and rest."
I feel His touch, my joys increase;
In Him there's hope, in Him there's peace.
I see His love, it's ev'rywhere.
How can I say, "God does not care"?

I do not know what lies ahead
But this I know, no fear, no dread
Shall rule my heart though dark the night
For Jesus is my Guide, my Light.

MY SHIP MUST WAIT

I don't know why my ship must wait
    Beside this sheltered shore
While other ships sail far across
    The ocean to explore;
I don't know why God laid His hand
    Upon the helm and said,
"Stay thou nearby" while others go
    So bravely on ahead.

But this I know, there is a thing
    Called Patience I must find
Somewhere within the harbor's sight
    Which others leave behind.
Yes, this I know, God plans the chart
    For captain and for crew;
And when I've learned my lesson well,
    Perhaps I'll sail on, too.

NOT ALL WE ASK

Not all we ask, but all we need
   God shall in truth supply;
Does He not clothe, does He not feed
   His own as time goes by?

Does He not send the sun, the rain,
   Ah yes, our daily bread?
Without His care we toil in vain —
   By His Hand we are fed.

Then why should we not be content
   With that which He may choose?
His greatest blessings shall be sent,
   No need shall He refuse.

Not all we ask, but all that's best
   He'll give from His great store;
How thankless, then, are we who test
   The latch which bars the door!

NOT MINE TO ASK

It is not mine to ask today
   Why this or that must be,
Why some dark cloud must hide the sun,
   Why pain should come to me.

It is but mine to say, "God is
   And somewhere in His plan
This, too, must have its rightful place
   Beyond the scope of man."

It is but mine to say, "Lead on,
   O precious Lord divine;
Some day I'll surely understand —
   Take Thou my hand in Thine."

ONE DAY AT A TIME

I do not need to live tomorrow, today;
For this, I thank the Lord each time I pray.

God knows that I'm not strong enough to bear
Twice as much of any joy or care;
Each day, each hour alike must have its share.

I do not need to live tomorrow, today,
Nor let today's cares into tomorrow stray.

One day at a time, well lived, can bring new power
To face whatever comes *when* comes tomorrow's hour;
One brick at a time can make a mighty tower.

I do not need to live tomorrow today;
God, in His infinite wisdom, planned it that way.

PERHAPS NOT ALL

Perhaps not all my heart shall want
  But all my heart shall need.
The Lord in mercy shall provide,
  All this, and more indeed.

He shall provide! God shall provide!
  I'm sure He knows what's best.
He shall provide! God shall provide!
  In Him, secure, I rest.

Perhaps not all my lips shall ask
  Of sun or skies of blue;
Perhaps not all, but this I know —
  God loves me through and through.

Perhaps not all or even half
  My dreams shall be fulfilled;
And yet, ah yes, God shall provide —
  All *good* things He has willed.

Perhaps not all I'd wish today
  But all each day *should* hold
The Lord shall surely send to me
  As all my days unfold.

He shall provide! God shall provide!
  I'm sure He knows what's best.
He shall provide! God shall provide!
  In Him, secure, I rest.

SAFE IN HIS CARE

Why do I feel that no one cares?
Why do I sit and sigh?
Why do I still refuse God's love
When He is standing by?

I'm never alone! Never alone!
Jesus, my Jesus, is near!
I'm never alone! Never alone!
Jesus, my Jesus, is near.

Why do I feel forsaken now
Despised by those I love?
Why do I fail to understand
God's watching from above?

Why do I feel that I alone
Must bear this grief and pain?
Why have I lost all faith and hope
Because God sent the rain?

Why do I feel the sun won't shine
When comes another day?
God sees each tear, He knows each need
And best is His own way.

I'm never alone! Never alone!
Jesus, my Jesus, is near.
I'm never alone! Never alone!
Jesus, my Jesus, is near.

SAIL ON

When troubles mount like ocean waves
    And sorrows dim your sight,
Know then God chastens whom He loves —
    Sail on, and trust His might.

Sail on! Sail on! The Lord is near!
    Have faith one moment more!
Sail on! Sail on and do not fear —
    He's waiting on the shore.

Somehow in God's all-perfect plan
    There must be winds and tide;
Sail on! Sail on, oh soul of man,
    His love is deep and wide.

Look up to Him, look up today,
    Your strength He shall renew;
Sail on though ceaseless be the storm —
    His love will see you through.

SHIP AHOY!

Leave your cargo of care over there
On the Isle of Despair and prepare
To rescue a brother;
Leave your doubting behind and come find
God's true peace of mind, the kind
You can share with another.

For many there be lost at sea
Just like you and like me, and we
Are about to sink
With the weight of the woe that we show
As our tears overflow. Heartaches grow,
Vision fails when we think
That *each* sails alone, that our own
Kind of grief is unknown. We bemoan
Our singular fate.
Rocks and reefs reach up high toward the sky,
Breakers roar, death seems nigh and we cry,
"Dear God, it's too late!"
But wait! Jesus bore His own store
Of such grief and much more before
His voyage was done;
And many there be lost at sea
Just like you and like me, and we
Are apart from none.

Go mend the rend in the sail of a friend!
Ship ahoy! Ship ahoy! Ship ahoy!

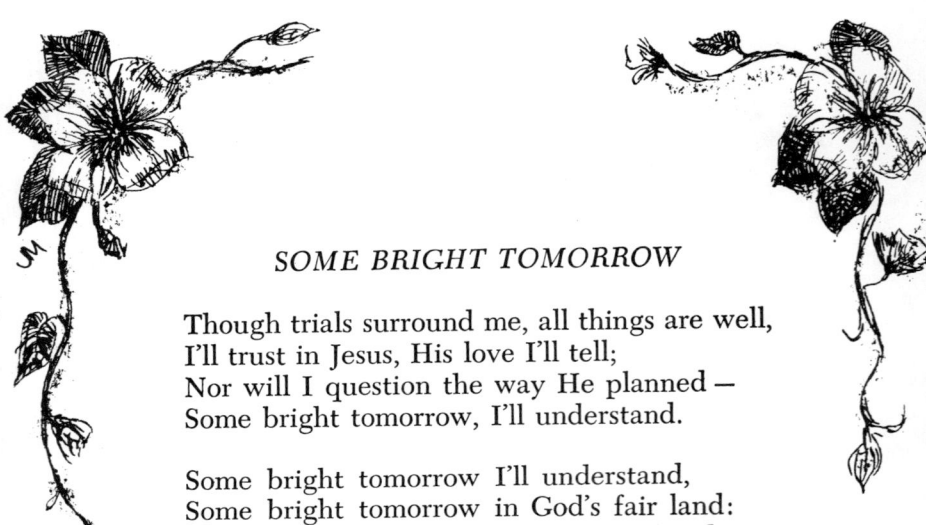

SOME BRIGHT TOMORROW

Though trials surround me, all things are well,
I'll trust in Jesus, His love I'll tell;
Nor will I question the way He planned —
Some bright tomorrow, I'll understand.

Some bright tomorrow I'll understand,
Some bright tomorrow in God's fair land:
I'll see and know Him, I'll touch His hand —
Some bright tomorrow, I'll understand.

When I'm discouraged, weary and sad,
I turn to Jesus, He makes me glad;
I have His promise some day He'll call —
Some bright tomorrow He'll tell me all.

Tears shall be ended all pain shall cease,
When I see Jesus, I'll find sweet peace;
There'll be no sorrow in heaven's strand —
Some bright tomorrow, I'll understand.

I'm looking forward to that bright day
When I shall vacate this house of clay;
I'll live with Jesus forevermore —
Some bright tomorrow inside the door.

Some bright tomorrow I'll understand,
Some bright tomorrow in God's fair land;
I'll see and know Him, I'll touch His hand —
Some bright tomorrow, I'll understand.

THE ANSWERED PRAYER

I prayed for cloudless skies and spring,
   For days without life's rain;
But God saw I could never grow
   Without my share of pain.

I prayed for love, for hope, for peace,
   And all things safe, secure;
But God willed I must understand
   What others must endure.

I prayed for health, oh, how I prayed!
   Days held so much to do;
But God saw fit to limit me
   In even this thing, too.

The task that He had planned for me
   Would need much thought, much prayer,
Much time to look to Him above,
   Much faith that I could share.

And so He sent the better thing
   Just as He always will;
If we but put our trust in Him,
   We'll find He loves us still.

THESE MUST BE BOUGHT

Don't try to change what you cannot change —
  Some things you must accept;
Some things God needs to temper souls —
  These must be bought and kept.

Just as roses need *both* sun and rain.
  We, too, need joy *and* pain;
Just as silver needs *both* heat and cold,
  We, too, need want *and* gold.

So work and plan from morn til night
  To keep each new day bright;
But *if* rain falls, and fall it must,
  Then learn to wait and trust.

Don't try to change what you cannot change —
  Some things you must accept;
Some things God needs to temper souls —
  These must be bought and kept.

THE TOUCH OF HIS HAND

So many times in so many ways
I've felt the touch of God's hand;
He lifted me, to Him be the praise —
I've felt the touch of His hand.

The touch of His hand! The touch of His hand!
I've felt the touch of God's hand!
My soul has been blessed, I've found perfect rest —
I've felt the touch of God's hand.

No matter when or how dark the night,
I've felt the touch of God's hand;
Each time He turned the darkness to light —
I've felt the touch of God's hand.

Though I must walk by faith, not by sight,
I've felt the touch of God's hand.
No fear have I, I'll trust in His might —
I've felt the touch of His hand.

The touch of His hand! The touch of His hand!
I've felt the touch of God's hand!
My soul has been blessed, I've found perfect rest,
I've felt the touch of God's hand.

THY WILL BE DONE, O LORD

Thy will be done?
Oh, can it be my stubborn self would run
Life's race without the guiding hand of One
Who knows
The heart's desire of ev'rything that grows,
Yes, even of each tiny little rose?

Has doubt begun?
Oh why should I fear to say Thy will be done
From rise, ah yes, and till the set of sun?
For who am I
That faith like the gossamer wings of a gay summer butterfly
Eludes my grasp each time as it flutters by?
Oh, my soul, resign!
Why should I fear to say Thy will not mine
When I am only human, God's divine?

WHY NOT TAKE IT ALL TO JESUS?

Why not take it all to Jesus?
Your poor soul will find relief.
Why not trust His tender mercy
And be free from all your grief?

Why not take it all to Jesus?
Why not let Him have His way?
He can see beyond tomorrow
And He'll send what's best today.

Why not take it all to Jesus?
There's no need to walk alone;
He is standing right beside you
And He cares for all His own.

Why not take it all to Jesus?
Why not let all doubting cease?
Let His blessing rest upon you
And you'll find God's perfect peace.

Oh, I come just now to Thee, Lord,
Fill my heart with peace and rest;
Mold my stubborn will, O Saviour,
Teach me now Thy way is best.

Oh, I come just now to Thee, Lord,
Take my heart and faith increase;
Let Thy blessing rest upon me —
Help me find Thy perfect peace.

WHY WORRY?

Why worry?
It never will gain you a thing.
The man that's worthwhile
Is the one who can smile
In winter the same as in spring.

Why worry?
You might just as well look up
And trust in the love
Of the Father above
As He bountifully fills your cup.

Why worry?
In faith and in hope ever dwell.
What seems like defeat
May be vict'ry complete —
God lives and all is well.

WITH A SONG IN MY HEART

Let me live with a song in my heart, dear Lord,
Give me faith as I kneel to pray;
Let me walk with true hope knowing Thy way is best,
There's a sun though the sky seems gray.

With a song in my heart, with a song in my heart,
Let me live with a song in my heart;
Let me trust day by day, truly trust as I pray,
Let me live with a song in my heart.

Let me live with a song in my heart, dear Lord,
Teach my soul to obey Thy will;
Just beyond ev'ry mountain of grief and woe
There's a valley of happiness still.

Let me live with a song in my heart, dear Lord,
Till this one bitter storm is past;
Though each moment seems now like a thousand years,
Let Thy love hold my anchor fast.

With a song in my heart, with a song in my heart,
Let me live with a song in my heart;
Let me trust day by day, truly trust as I pray —
Let me live with a song in my heart.

WHO AM I?

Who am I
That I should fail to trust God's will?
Who am I
That I should even ask Him why?
Who am I
That I should choose to doubt God still?
Who am I?
Who am I?

Who am I
That I should fail to pass God's test?
Who am I
That I should even breathe one sigh?
Who am I
That I should think my way was best?
Who am I?
Who am I?